# 50 Supreme Chocolate Dessert Lovers Recipes

By: Kelly Johnson

# Table of Contents

- Chocolate Lava Cake
- Death by Chocolate Cake
- Chocolate Mousse
- Brownies with Walnuts
- Chocolate Chip Cookies
- Chocolate Cheesecake
- Chocolate Fondue
- Chocolate Pudding Pie
- Chocolate Eclairs
- Nutella Swirl Brownies
- Chocolate Fudge Cake
- Double Chocolate Chip Muffins
- Chocolate Truffles
- Molten Chocolate Cupcakes
- Chocolate Soufflé
- Chocolate Raspberry Tart
- Chocolate Peanut Butter Pie
- Chocolate Coconut Macaroons
- Chocolate Covered Strawberries
- Rocky Road Ice Cream
- Chocolate Almond Biscotti
- Chocolate Cream Pie
- Chocolate Hazelnut Spread Brownies
- Chocolate Orange Tart
- Chocolate Chip Pancakes
- Chocolate Tiramisu
- Chocolate Fudge Brownies
- White Chocolate Raspberry Cheesecake
- Chocolate Covered Pretzels
- Chocolate Peanut Butter Cups
- Chocolate Chip Scones
- Chocolate Crinkle Cookies
- Chocolate Almond Joy Bars
- Chocolate Swirl Pound Cake
- Chocolate Cherry Brownies

- Chocolate Mint Mousse
- Chocolate Cheesecake Brownies
- S'mores Dip
- Chocolate Dipped Oreos
- Chocolate Chip Banana Bread
- Chocolate Cake Pops
- Chocolate Waffles
- Chocolate Peanut Butter Smoothie Bowl
- Chocolate Silk Pie
- Chocolate Caramel Tart
- Chocolate Chia Seed Pudding
- Chocolate Hazelnut Mousse
- Chocolate Banana Cream Pie
- Chocolate Ganache Tart
- Chocolate Flan

# Chocolate Lava Cake

**Ingredients**

- 1 cup semi-sweet chocolate chips
- ½ cup unsalted butter
- 1 cup powdered sugar
- 2 large eggs
- 2 large egg yolks
- 1 teaspoon vanilla extract
- ½ cup all-purpose flour
- Pinch of salt

**Instructions**

1. **Preheat Oven:**
    - Preheat oven to 425°F (220°C). Grease four ramekins and place them on a baking sheet.
2. **Melt Chocolate and Butter:**
    - In a microwave-safe bowl, melt chocolate chips and butter together until smooth. Stir in powdered sugar.
3. **Add Eggs and Flour:**
    - Whisk in eggs and egg yolks until combined. Stir in vanilla, flour, and salt until just combined.
4. **Bake:**
    - Divide the batter among the ramekins. Bake for 12-14 minutes until the edges are firm but the center is soft. Let cool for 1 minute, then invert onto plates. Serve warm.

## Death by Chocolate Cake

**Ingredients**

- 1 ¾ cups all-purpose flour
- 2 cups granulated sugar
- ¾ cup unsweetened cocoa powder
- 1 ½ teaspoons baking powder
- 1 ½ teaspoons baking soda
- 1 teaspoon salt
- 2 large eggs
- 1 cup whole milk
- ½ cup vegetable oil
- 2 teaspoons vanilla extract
- 1 cup boiling water
- Chocolate frosting (for layering)

**Instructions**

1. **Preheat Oven:**
   - Preheat oven to 350°F (175°C). Grease and flour two 9-inch round cake pans.
2. **Mix Dry Ingredients:**
   - In a large bowl, combine flour, sugar, cocoa powder, baking powder, baking soda, and salt.
3. **Combine Wet Ingredients:**
   - Add eggs, milk, oil, and vanilla. Mix on medium speed for 2 minutes. Stir in boiling water until well combined.
4. **Bake:**
   - Pour batter evenly into the prepared pans. Bake for 30-35 minutes. Let cool in the pans for 10 minutes, then transfer to wire racks to cool completely.
5. **Layer and Frost:**
   - Once cooled, layer the cakes with chocolate frosting in between and on top.

## Chocolate Mousse

**Ingredients**

- 1 cup semi-sweet chocolate chips
- 2 tablespoons unsalted butter
- 3 large eggs, separated
- ¼ cup granulated sugar
- 1 cup heavy cream
- 1 teaspoon vanilla extract

**Instructions**

1. **Melt Chocolate:**
    - In a microwave-safe bowl, melt chocolate chips and butter until smooth. Allow to cool slightly.
2. **Whisk Egg Yolks:**
    - In a separate bowl, whisk egg yolks and sugar until thick and pale. Stir in the melted chocolate and vanilla.
3. **Beat Egg Whites:**
    - In another bowl, beat egg whites until stiff peaks form. Gently fold into the chocolate mixture.
4. **Whip Cream:**
    - In a separate bowl, whip heavy cream until soft peaks form. Fold into the chocolate mixture until fully combined.
5. **Chill:**
    - Spoon mousse into serving dishes and refrigerate for at least 2 hours before serving.

## Brownies with Walnuts

### Ingredients

- 1 cup unsalted butter
- 2 cups granulated sugar
- 4 large eggs
- 1 teaspoon vanilla extract
- 1 cup all-purpose flour
- ½ cup unsweetened cocoa powder
- ½ teaspoon salt
- 1 cup walnuts, chopped

### Instructions

1. **Preheat Oven:**
    - Preheat oven to 350°F (175°C). Grease a 9x13 inch baking dish.
2. **Melt Butter:**
    - In a saucepan, melt butter over low heat. Remove from heat and stir in sugar, eggs, and vanilla.
3. **Mix Dry Ingredients:**
    - Combine flour, cocoa powder, and salt. Stir into the butter mixture until well combined. Fold in walnuts.
4. **Bake:**
    - Pour the batter into the prepared baking dish. Bake for 20-25 minutes. Let cool before cutting into squares.

# Chocolate Chip Cookies

**Ingredients**

- 2 ¼ cups all-purpose flour
- 1 teaspoon baking soda
- ½ teaspoon salt
- 1 cup unsalted butter, softened
- ¾ cup granulated sugar
- ¾ cup brown sugar
- 1 teaspoon vanilla extract
- 2 large eggs
- 2 cups semi-sweet chocolate chips

**Instructions**

1. **Preheat Oven:**
   - Preheat oven to 375°F (190°C). Line baking sheets with parchment paper.
2. **Mix Dry Ingredients:**
   - In a small bowl, combine flour, baking soda, and salt.
3. **Cream Butter and Sugars:**
   - In a large bowl, cream together butter, granulated sugar, brown sugar, and vanilla until smooth. Beat in eggs one at a time.
4. **Combine Mixtures:**
   - Gradually blend in the flour mixture. Stir in chocolate chips.
5. **Bake:**
   - Drop by rounded tablespoon onto prepared baking sheets. Bake for 9-11 minutes until golden brown. Let cool on wire racks.

# Chocolate Cheesecake

**Ingredients**

- 1 ½ cups graham cracker crumbs
- ½ cup unsalted butter, melted
- 1 cup granulated sugar
- 2 (8-ounce) packages cream cheese, softened
- 1 cup semi-sweet chocolate chips, melted
- 3 large eggs
- 1 teaspoon vanilla extract

**Instructions**

1. **Preheat Oven:**
    - Preheat oven to 325°F (160°C). Grease a 9-inch springform pan.
2. **Make Crust:**
    - In a bowl, combine graham cracker crumbs and melted butter. Press mixture into the bottom of the pan.
3. **Mix Filling:**
    - In a large bowl, beat cream cheese and sugar until smooth. Blend in melted chocolate, then add eggs one at a time, mixing well after each addition. Stir in vanilla.
4. **Bake:**
    - Pour filling over the crust. Bake for 55-60 minutes until set. Let cool, then refrigerate for at least 4 hours before serving.

## Chocolate Fondue

**Ingredients**

- 8 ounces semi-sweet chocolate, chopped
- 1 cup heavy cream
- 1 teaspoon vanilla extract
- Fresh fruits, marshmallows, and pretzels (for dipping)

**Instructions**

1. **Heat Cream:**
    - In a saucepan, heat heavy cream over medium heat until hot but not boiling.
2. **Melt Chocolate:**
    - Remove from heat and add chopped chocolate and vanilla. Stir until melted and smooth.
3. **Serve:**
    - Transfer to a fondue pot or bowl. Serve with fresh fruits, marshmallows, and pretzels for dipping.

# Chocolate Pudding Pie

## Ingredients

- 1 pre-baked pie crust
- 1 cup milk
- ½ cup granulated sugar
- ⅓ cup unsweetened cocoa powder
- 3 tablespoons cornstarch
- ¼ teaspoon salt
- 2 tablespoons unsalted butter
- 1 teaspoon vanilla extract
- Whipped cream (for topping)

## Instructions

1. **Make Pudding:**
   - In a saucepan, whisk together milk, sugar, cocoa powder, cornstarch, and salt. Cook over medium heat, stirring constantly until thickened and bubbly.
2. **Finish Pudding:**
   - Remove from heat and stir in butter and vanilla until smooth. Pour into the pre-baked pie crust.
3. **Chill:**
   - Refrigerate for at least 2 hours. Top with whipped cream before serving.

# Chocolate Eclairs

**Ingredients**

- **For the Choux Pastry:**
    - 1 cup water
    - ½ cup unsalted butter
    - 1 cup all-purpose flour
    - 4 large eggs
    - 1 teaspoon vanilla extract
    - Pinch of salt
- **For the Pastry Cream:**
    - 2 cups milk
    - ½ cup granulated sugar
    - 1/3 cup cornstarch
    - 4 large egg yolks
    - 2 tablespoons unsalted butter
    - 1 teaspoon vanilla extract
- **For the Chocolate Glaze:**
    - 4 ounces semi-sweet chocolate, chopped
    - ½ cup heavy cream

**Instructions**

1. **Make the Choux Pastry:**
    - Preheat oven to 400°F (200°C). In a saucepan, bring water, butter, and salt to a boil. Remove from heat and stir in flour until combined. Add eggs one at a time, mixing until smooth.
2. **Pipe the Pastry:**
    - Transfer the dough to a piping bag and pipe 4-inch strips onto a lined baking sheet. Bake for 25-30 minutes until golden. Let cool completely.
3. **Prepare the Pastry Cream:**
    - In a saucepan, heat milk and sugar until simmering. In a bowl, whisk together cornstarch and egg yolks. Gradually add hot milk mixture, then return to the saucepan and cook until thickened. Stir in butter and vanilla. Cool completely.
4. **Fill Eclairs:**
    - Once cool, fill eclairs with pastry cream using a piping bag.
5. **Make the Chocolate Glaze:**

- Heat cream until just simmering. Pour over chocolate and stir until smooth. Dip the tops of eclairs in the glaze and allow to set.

## Nutella Swirl Brownies

### Ingredients

- 1 cup unsalted butter
- 2 cups granulated sugar
- 4 large eggs
- 1 teaspoon vanilla extract
- 1 cup all-purpose flour
- ½ cup unsweetened cocoa powder
- ½ teaspoon salt
- 1 cup Nutella

### Instructions

1. **Preheat Oven:**
   - Preheat oven to 350°F (175°C). Grease a 9x13 inch baking pan.
2. **Mix Wet Ingredients:**
   - In a large bowl, melt butter and mix with sugar. Add eggs and vanilla, mixing well.
3. **Add Dry Ingredients:**
   - Stir in flour, cocoa powder, and salt until just combined.
4. **Swirl in Nutella:**
   - Pour half the brownie batter into the pan. Drop spoonfuls of Nutella on top and swirl with a knife. Add remaining batter and repeat the Nutella swirl.
5. **Bake:**
   - Bake for 25-30 minutes until a toothpick inserted comes out with moist crumbs. Let cool before cutting into squares.

## Chocolate Fudge Cake

**Ingredients**

- 1 ¾ cups all-purpose flour
- 2 cups granulated sugar
- ¾ cup unsweetened cocoa powder
- 1 ½ teaspoons baking powder
- 1 ½ teaspoons baking soda
- 1 teaspoon salt
- 2 large eggs
- 1 cup whole milk
- ½ cup vegetable oil
- 2 teaspoons vanilla extract
- 1 cup boiling water

**Instructions**

1. **Preheat Oven:**
    - Preheat oven to 350°F (175°C). Grease and flour two 9-inch round cake pans.
2. **Mix Dry Ingredients:**
    - In a large bowl, combine flour, sugar, cocoa powder, baking powder, baking soda, and salt.
3. **Combine Wet Ingredients:**
    - Add eggs, milk, oil, and vanilla. Mix on medium speed for 2 minutes. Stir in boiling water until well combined.
4. **Bake:**
    - Divide the batter evenly into the prepared pans. Bake for 30-35 minutes. Let cool in pans for 10 minutes, then transfer to wire racks to cool completely.

# Double Chocolate Chip Muffins

**Ingredients**

- 1 ½ cups all-purpose flour
- ½ cup unsweetened cocoa powder
- 1 cup granulated sugar
- 2 teaspoons baking powder
- ½ teaspoon baking soda
- ½ teaspoon salt
- 2 large eggs
- 1 cup milk
- ½ cup vegetable oil
- 1 cup semi-sweet chocolate chips

**Instructions**

1. **Preheat Oven:**
    - Preheat oven to 350°F (175°C). Line a muffin tin with paper liners.
2. **Mix Dry Ingredients:**
    - In a large bowl, combine flour, cocoa powder, sugar, baking powder, baking soda, and salt.
3. **Combine Wet Ingredients:**
    - In another bowl, whisk together eggs, milk, and oil. Add to dry ingredients and mix until just combined. Fold in chocolate chips.
4. **Bake:**
    - Divide batter among muffin cups. Bake for 20-25 minutes until a toothpick inserted comes out clean. Cool before serving.

## Chocolate Truffles

**Ingredients**

- 8 ounces semi-sweet chocolate, chopped
- ½ cup heavy cream
- 1 teaspoon vanilla extract
- Cocoa powder, crushed nuts, or sprinkles (for rolling)

**Instructions**

1. **Melt Chocolate:**
   - In a heatproof bowl, combine chocolate and cream. Heat over a double boiler or microwave until melted and smooth. Stir in vanilla.
2. **Chill Mixture:**
   - Refrigerate for 1-2 hours until firm enough to scoop.
3. **Form Truffles:**
   - Using a small cookie scoop or your hands, form balls from the chocolate mixture. Roll in cocoa powder, nuts, or sprinkles.
4. **Chill Again:**
   - Place truffles on a lined baking sheet and refrigerate until set.

# Molten Chocolate Cupcakes

## Ingredients

- ½ cup unsalted butter
- 1 cup semi-sweet chocolate chips
- 2 large eggs
- 2 large egg yolks
- ¼ cup granulated sugar
- 2 tablespoons all-purpose flour
- Pinch of salt

## Instructions

1. **Preheat Oven:**
    - Preheat oven to 425°F (220°C). Grease four ramekins.
2. **Melt Chocolate:**
    - In a microwave-safe bowl, melt butter and chocolate together until smooth.
3. **Mix Eggs and Sugar:**
    - In a separate bowl, whisk together eggs, egg yolks, and sugar until thick. Stir in the melted chocolate mixture.
4. **Add Flour and Bake:**
    - Stir in flour and salt. Divide the batter among ramekins. Bake for 12-14 minutes until the edges are firm but the center is soft.
5. **Serve:**
    - Let cool for 1 minute, then invert onto plates and serve warm.

# Chocolate Soufflé

**Ingredients**

- 2 tablespoons unsalted butter (for greasing)
- 2 tablespoons granulated sugar (for dusting)
- 6 ounces semi-sweet chocolate, chopped
- 3 large eggs, separated
- ¼ cup granulated sugar
- 1 teaspoon vanilla extract
- Pinch of salt

**Instructions**

1. **Preheat Oven:**
    - Preheat oven to 375°F (190°C). Grease and dust four ramekins with sugar.
2. **Melt Chocolate:**
    - In a double boiler, melt chocolate. Remove from heat and let cool slightly.
3. **Beat Egg Yolks:**
    - In a bowl, beat egg yolks and ¼ cup sugar until pale. Stir in melted chocolate and vanilla.
4. **Beat Egg Whites:**
    - In a separate bowl, beat egg whites and salt until stiff peaks form. Gently fold into the chocolate mixture.
5. **Bake:**
    - Pour the mixture into the prepared ramekins and bake for 12-15 minutes until puffed. Serve immediately.

# Chocolate Raspberry Tart

**Ingredients**

- **For the Crust:**
    - 1 ½ cups graham cracker crumbs
    - ½ cup unsalted butter, melted
    - ¼ cup granulated sugar
- **For the Filling:**
    - 8 ounces semi-sweet chocolate, chopped
    - 1 cup heavy cream
    - 2 tablespoons unsalted butter
    - 1 teaspoon vanilla extract
    - 1 cup fresh raspberries

**Instructions**

1. **Preheat Oven:**
    - Preheat oven to 350°F (175°C). In a bowl, combine crust ingredients. Press into the bottom of a tart pan.
2. **Bake Crust:**
    - Bake for 8-10 minutes until golden. Let cool.
3. **Make Filling:**
    - In a saucepan, heat cream until simmering. Pour over chocolate and let sit for a few minutes. Stir in butter and vanilla until smooth.
4. **Assemble Tart:**
    - Pour chocolate filling into the cooled crust and top with raspberries. Refrigerate for at least 2 hours before serving.

# Chocolate Peanut Butter Pie

**Ingredients**

- **For the Crust:**
    - 1 ½ cups graham cracker crumbs
    - ½ cup unsalted butter, melted
    - ¼ cup granulated sugar
- **For the Filling:**
    - 1 cup creamy peanut butter
    - 1 cup powdered sugar
    - 8 ounces cream cheese, softened
    - 1 cup heavy cream
    - ½ teaspoon vanilla extract
- **For the Topping:**
    - 4 ounces semi-sweet chocolate, chopped
    - ½ cup heavy cream

**Instructions**

1. **Preheat Oven:**
    - Preheat oven to 350°F (175°C). Combine crust ingredients and press into a pie pan. Bake for 8-10 minutes.
2. **Prepare Filling:**
    - In a bowl, beat peanut butter, powdered sugar, and cream cheese until smooth. In another bowl, whip heavy cream and vanilla until stiff peaks form. Fold into peanut butter mixture.
3. **Assemble Pie:**
    - Pour filling into cooled crust and smooth the top. Refrigerate for at least 4 hours.
4. **Make Chocolate Topping:**
    - Heat ½ cup cream until simmering. Pour over chocolate and stir until smooth. Let cool slightly, then pour over pie. Chill until set.

# Chocolate Coconut Macaroons

## Ingredients

- 3 cups sweetened shredded coconut
- 2/3 cup sweetened condensed milk
- 1 teaspoon vanilla extract
- 2 large egg whites
- 1/4 teaspoon salt
- 8 ounces semi-sweet chocolate, chopped (for dipping)

## Instructions

1. **Preheat Oven:**
   - Preheat the oven to 325°F (160°C) and line a baking sheet with parchment paper.
2. **Mix Ingredients:**
   - In a bowl, combine shredded coconut, sweetened condensed milk, and vanilla extract. In another bowl, beat the egg whites and salt until soft peaks form, then gently fold them into the coconut mixture.
3. **Shape Macaroons:**
   - Drop rounded tablespoons of the mixture onto the prepared baking sheet.
4. **Bake:**
   - Bake for 20-25 minutes, or until the tops are golden brown. Let cool completely.
5. **Dip in Chocolate:**
   - Melt the chocolate and dip the bottoms of the cooled macaroons into it. Place back on parchment to set.

# Chocolate Covered Strawberries

## Ingredients

- 1 pound fresh strawberries, washed and dried
- 8 ounces semi-sweet chocolate, chopped
- 1 tablespoon coconut oil (optional, for shine)

## Instructions

1. **Prepare Strawberries:**
    - Ensure strawberries are completely dry.
2. **Melt Chocolate:**
    - In a microwave-safe bowl, combine chocolate and coconut oil. Heat in 30-second intervals until melted and smooth, stirring between intervals.
3. **Dip Strawberries:**
    - Dip each strawberry into the melted chocolate, allowing excess to drip off.
4. **Set:**
    - Place dipped strawberries on a parchment-lined tray. Refrigerate until the chocolate is set.

## Rocky Road Ice Cream

### Ingredients

- 2 cups heavy cream
- 1 cup sweetened condensed milk
- 1 teaspoon vanilla extract
- 1/2 cup mini marshmallows
- 1/2 cup chopped nuts (walnuts or almonds)
- 1/2 cup chocolate chips or chunks

### Instructions

1. **Mix Base:**
   - In a bowl, whisk together heavy cream, sweetened condensed milk, and vanilla until well combined.
2. **Add Mix-ins:**
   - Fold in mini marshmallows, nuts, and chocolate chips.
3. **Chill:**
   - Pour the mixture into a freezer-safe container and freeze for at least 6 hours or until firm.

## Chocolate Almond Biscotti

**Ingredients**

- 2 cups all-purpose flour
- 1 cup granulated sugar
- 1/2 cup unsweetened cocoa powder
- 1 teaspoon baking powder
- 1/4 teaspoon salt
- 3 large eggs
- 1 teaspoon vanilla extract
- 1 cup chopped almonds
- 4 ounces semi-sweet chocolate, melted (for drizzling)

**Instructions**

1. **Preheat Oven:**
    - Preheat the oven to 350°F (175°C). Line a baking sheet with parchment paper.
2. **Mix Dry Ingredients:**
    - In a bowl, combine flour, sugar, cocoa powder, baking powder, and salt.
3. **Add Wet Ingredients:**
    - In another bowl, whisk eggs and vanilla. Combine with dry ingredients. Fold in almonds.
4. **Shape and Bake:**
    - Form dough into a log on the baking sheet and bake for 25 minutes. Let cool, then slice into 1-inch pieces.
5. **Second Bake:**
    - Return sliced biscotti to the oven and bake for an additional 10-15 minutes. Let cool, then drizzle with melted chocolate.

# Chocolate Cream Pie

**Ingredients**

- **For the Crust:**
    - 1 ½ cups graham cracker crumbs
    - ½ cup unsalted butter, melted
    - ¼ cup granulated sugar
- **For the Filling:**
    - 1/3 cup granulated sugar
    - 1/4 cup unsweetened cocoa powder
    - 3 tablespoons cornstarch
    - 1/8 teaspoon salt
    - 2 cups whole milk
    - 2 large egg yolks
    - 1 teaspoon vanilla extract
    - 2 tablespoons unsalted butter
    - Whipped cream (for topping)

**Instructions**

1. **Prepare Crust:**
    - Preheat oven to 350°F (175°C). Combine crust ingredients and press into a pie pan. Bake for 8-10 minutes. Let cool.
2. **Make Filling:**
    - In a saucepan, whisk together sugar, cocoa powder, cornstarch, and salt. Gradually whisk in milk. Cook over medium heat until thickened. Stir in egg yolks, vanilla, and butter.
3. **Assemble Pie:**
    - Pour filling into the cooled crust. Refrigerate for at least 4 hours. Top with whipped cream before serving.

# Chocolate Hazelnut Spread Brownies

## Ingredients

- 1 cup unsalted butter
- 1 cup granulated sugar
- 4 large eggs
- 1 teaspoon vanilla extract
- 1 cup all-purpose flour
- 1/2 cup unsweetened cocoa powder
- 1/2 teaspoon salt
- 1 cup chocolate hazelnut spread (like Nutella)

## Instructions

1. **Preheat Oven:**
   - Preheat oven to 350°F (175°C). Grease a 9x13 inch baking pan.
2. **Mix Wet Ingredients:**
   - In a saucepan, melt butter. Stir in sugar, then add eggs and vanilla, mixing well.
3. **Add Dry Ingredients:**
   - Stir in flour, cocoa powder, and salt until just combined. Fold in hazelnut spread.
4. **Bake:**
   - Pour into the prepared pan and bake for 25-30 minutes. Let cool before cutting into squares.

# Chocolate Orange Tart

**Ingredients**

- **For the Crust:**
    - 1 ½ cups chocolate cookie crumbs
    - ½ cup unsalted butter, melted
- **For the Filling:**
    - 8 ounces semi-sweet chocolate, chopped
    - 1 cup heavy cream
    - Zest of 1 orange
    - 1/4 cup fresh orange juice
    - 2 large eggs

**Instructions**

1. **Preheat Oven:**
    - Preheat the oven to 350°F (175°C). Combine crust ingredients and press into a tart pan. Bake for 10 minutes and let cool.
2. **Prepare Filling:**
    - In a saucepan, heat cream until simmering. Pour over chopped chocolate and let sit until melted. Stir in orange zest and juice.
3. **Combine with Eggs:**
    - Whisk in eggs until smooth. Pour filling into the cooled crust.
4. **Bake:**
    - Bake for 25-30 minutes until set. Let cool before slicing.

# Chocolate Chip Pancakes

**Ingredients**

- 1 cup all-purpose flour
- 2 tablespoons granulated sugar
- 2 teaspoons baking powder
- 1/2 teaspoon salt
- 1 cup milk
- 1 large egg
- 2 tablespoons melted butter
- 1/2 cup chocolate chips

**Instructions**

1. **Mix Dry Ingredients:**
    - In a bowl, whisk together flour, sugar, baking powder, and salt.
2. **Add Wet Ingredients:**
    - In another bowl, combine milk, egg, and melted butter. Mix into dry ingredients until just combined. Fold in chocolate chips.
3. **Cook Pancakes:**
    - Heat a skillet over medium heat. Pour batter onto the skillet and cook until bubbles form. Flip and cook until golden brown on both sides.

## Chocolate Tiramisu

### Ingredients

- 1 cup strong brewed coffee, cooled
- 1/2 cup coffee liqueur (optional)
- 8 ounces mascarpone cheese
- 1 cup heavy cream
- 1/2 cup granulated sugar
- 1 teaspoon vanilla extract
- 24 ladyfinger cookies
- Unsweetened cocoa powder (for dusting)

### Instructions

1. **Prepare Coffee Mixture:**
   - Combine brewed coffee and coffee liqueur in a shallow dish.
2. **Make Filling:**
   - In a bowl, whisk mascarpone, heavy cream, sugar, and vanilla until soft peaks form.
3. **Assemble:**
   - Dip ladyfingers in the coffee mixture and layer in a dish. Spread half of the mascarpone mixture on top. Repeat layers and finish with remaining filling.
4. **Chill:**
   - Refrigerate for at least 4 hours. Dust with cocoa powder before serving.

## Chocolate Fudge Brownies

**Ingredients**

- 1/2 cup unsalted butter
- 1 cup granulated sugar
- 2 large eggs
- 1 teaspoon vanilla extract
- 1/3 cup unsweetened cocoa powder
- 1 cup all-purpose flour
- 1/4 teaspoon salt
- 1/4 teaspoon baking powder

**Instructions**

1. **Preheat Oven:**
   - Preheat the oven to 350°F (175°C). Grease a 9x9-inch baking pan.
2. **Melt Butter:**
   - In a saucepan, melt the butter. Remove from heat and stir in sugar, eggs, and vanilla.
3. **Combine Dry Ingredients:**
   - Mix in cocoa, flour, salt, and baking powder until just combined.
4. **Bake:**
   - Pour the batter into the prepared pan and bake for 20-25 minutes. Let cool before cutting into squares.

# White Chocolate Raspberry Cheesecake

**Ingredients**

- **For the Crust:**
    - 1 1/2 cups graham cracker crumbs
    - 1/4 cup granulated sugar
    - 1/2 cup unsalted butter, melted
- **For the Filling:**
    - 16 ounces cream cheese, softened
    - 3/4 cup granulated sugar
    - 3 large eggs
    - 1 teaspoon vanilla extract
    - 8 ounces white chocolate, melted
    - 1 cup fresh raspberries

**Instructions**

1. **Preheat Oven:**
    - Preheat the oven to 325°F (160°C). Combine crust ingredients and press into a 9-inch springform pan. Bake for 10 minutes and let cool.
2. **Make Filling:**
    - In a bowl, beat cream cheese and sugar until smooth. Add eggs one at a time, mixing well. Stir in vanilla and melted white chocolate.
3. **Add Raspberries:**
    - Fold in fresh raspberries gently.
4. **Bake:**
    - Pour filling into the crust and bake for 50-60 minutes. Let cool and refrigerate for at least 4 hours before serving.

# Chocolate Covered Pretzels

**Ingredients**

- 1 cup semi-sweet chocolate chips
- 1 cup mini pretzels
- 1/2 cup white chocolate chips (optional, for drizzling)

**Instructions**

1. **Melt Chocolate:**
    - In a microwave-safe bowl, melt semi-sweet chocolate chips in 30-second intervals, stirring until smooth.
2. **Dip Pretzels:**
    - Dip each pretzel into melted chocolate, allowing excess to drip off. Place on a parchment-lined tray.
3. **Optional Drizzle:**
    - Melt white chocolate chips and drizzle over the coated pretzels.
4. **Set:**
    - Refrigerate until chocolate is set.

## Chocolate Peanut Butter Cups

**Ingredients**

- 1 cup semi-sweet chocolate chips
- 1/2 cup creamy peanut butter
- 1/4 cup powdered sugar
- Mini muffin liners

**Instructions**

1. **Melt Chocolate:**
    - Melt chocolate chips in a microwave-safe bowl, stirring until smooth.
2. **Prepare Muffin Liners:**
    - Place mini muffin liners in a muffin tin. Spoon a small amount of melted chocolate into each liner and spread it up the sides.
3. **Make Filling:**
    - In a bowl, mix peanut butter and powdered sugar until smooth. Spoon the mixture into each chocolate-lined cup.
4. **Top with Chocolate:**
    - Pour remaining melted chocolate over the peanut butter filling to cover.
5. **Chill:**
    - Refrigerate until set.

# Chocolate Chip Scones

**Ingredients**

- 2 cups all-purpose flour
- 1/4 cup granulated sugar
- 1 tablespoon baking powder
- 1/2 teaspoon salt
- 1/2 cup unsalted butter, cold and cubed
- 1/2 cup heavy cream
- 1 large egg
- 1 cup chocolate chips

**Instructions**

1. **Preheat Oven:**
   - Preheat the oven to 400°F (200°C). Line a baking sheet with parchment paper.
2. **Combine Dry Ingredients:**
   - In a bowl, whisk together flour, sugar, baking powder, and salt. Cut in butter until the mixture resembles coarse crumbs.
3. **Mix Wet Ingredients:**
   - In another bowl, mix heavy cream and egg. Stir into the dry mixture until just combined. Fold in chocolate chips.
4. **Shape Scones:**
   - Turn dough onto a floured surface and shape into a circle about 1 inch thick. Cut into wedges and place on the baking sheet.
5. **Bake:**
   - Bake for 15-20 minutes until golden brown. Let cool slightly before serving.

# Chocolate Crinkle Cookies

**Ingredients**

- 1 cup semi-sweet chocolate chips
- 1/4 cup unsweetened cocoa powder
- 1 cup granulated sugar
- 1/4 cup vegetable oil
- 2 large eggs
- 1 teaspoon vanilla extract
- 1 cup all-purpose flour
- 1/2 teaspoon baking powder
- 1/4 teaspoon salt
- Powdered sugar (for rolling)

**Instructions**

1. **Melt Chocolate:**
   - Melt chocolate chips in a microwave-safe bowl. Let cool slightly.
2. **Mix Ingredients:**
   - In a bowl, combine melted chocolate, cocoa powder, sugar, oil, eggs, and vanilla. Stir until smooth. Add flour, baking powder, and salt; mix until combined.
3. **Chill Dough:**
   - Chill dough in the refrigerator for at least 30 minutes.
4. **Preheat Oven:**
   - Preheat oven to 350°F (175°C). Line a baking sheet with parchment paper.
5. **Form Cookies:**
   - Scoop dough and roll into balls. Roll in powdered sugar to coat.
6. **Bake:**
   - Place on baking sheet and bake for 10-12 minutes. Let cool before serving.

## Chocolate Almond Joy Bars

**Ingredients**

- **For the Base:**
    - 1 cup almond flour
    - 1/4 cup unsweetened cocoa powder
    - 1/4 cup maple syrup
    - 1/4 cup coconut oil, melted
    - 1/2 teaspoon vanilla extract
    - 1/4 teaspoon salt
- **For the Topping:**
    - 1 cup shredded coconut
    - 1/2 cup almonds, chopped
    - 8 ounces dark chocolate, chopped (for coating)

**Instructions**

1. **Prepare Base:**
    - In a bowl, mix almond flour, cocoa powder, maple syrup, coconut oil, vanilla, and salt until combined. Press mixture into an 8x8-inch pan lined with parchment paper.
2. **Add Topping:**
    - Sprinkle shredded coconut and chopped almonds evenly over the base.
3. **Melt Chocolate:**
    - Melt dark chocolate and pour over the top, spreading evenly.
4. **Chill:**
    - Refrigerate until firm, then cut into bars.

# Chocolate Swirl Pound Cake

**Ingredients**

- 1 cup unsalted butter, softened
- 2 cups granulated sugar
- 4 large eggs
- 2 teaspoons vanilla extract
- 3 cups all-purpose flour
- 1 teaspoon baking powder
- 1/2 teaspoon salt
- 1 cup sour cream
- 1/2 cup unsweetened cocoa powder

**Instructions**

1. **Preheat Oven:**
   - Preheat the oven to 350°F (175°C). Grease and flour a loaf pan.
2. **Cream Butter and Sugar:**
   - In a bowl, cream together butter and sugar until light and fluffy. Beat in eggs one at a time, then stir in vanilla.
3. **Mix Dry Ingredients:**
   - In another bowl, mix flour, baking powder, and salt. Gradually add to the creamed mixture alternately with sour cream.
4. **Divide and Swirl:**
   - Divide the batter in half. Mix cocoa powder into one half. Alternate spooning the batters into the prepared pan and swirl with a knife.
5. **Bake:**
   - Bake for 60-70 minutes or until a toothpick comes out clean. Let cool before slicing.

# Chocolate Cherry Brownies

## Ingredients

- 1/2 cup unsalted butter
- 1 cup granulated sugar
- 2 large eggs
- 1 teaspoon vanilla extract
- 1/3 cup unsweetened cocoa powder
- 1 cup all-purpose flour
- 1/4 teaspoon salt
- 1/4 teaspoon baking powder
- 1 cup pitted cherries, chopped (fresh or frozen)

## Instructions

1. **Preheat Oven:**
    - Preheat the oven to 350°F (175°C). Grease an 8x8-inch baking pan.
2. **Melt Butter:**
    - In a saucepan, melt the butter. Remove from heat and stir in sugar, eggs, and vanilla.
3. **Combine Dry Ingredients:**
    - Mix in cocoa, flour, salt, and baking powder until just combined. Fold in chopped cherries.
4. **Bake:**
    - Pour the batter into the prepared pan and bake for 20-25 minutes. Let cool before cutting into squares.

## Chocolate Mint Mousse

**Ingredients**

- 1 cup semi-sweet chocolate chips
- 2 tablespoons unsalted butter
- 1 teaspoon peppermint extract
- 2 cups heavy cream
- 1/4 cup powdered sugar

**Instructions**

1. **Melt Chocolate:**
    - In a microwave-safe bowl, melt chocolate chips and butter in 30-second intervals, stirring until smooth. Stir in peppermint extract and let cool slightly.
2. **Whip Cream:**
    - In a separate bowl, whip heavy cream and powdered sugar until soft peaks form.
3. **Combine:**
    - Gently fold the whipped cream into the chocolate mixture until fully combined.
4. **Chill:**
    - Spoon mousse into serving dishes and refrigerate for at least 2 hours before serving.

# Chocolate Cheesecake Brownies

## Ingredients

- **For the Brownies:**
    - 1/2 cup unsalted butter
    - 1 cup granulated sugar
    - 2 large eggs
    - 1 teaspoon vanilla extract
    - 1/3 cup unsweetened cocoa powder
    - 1 cup all-purpose flour
    - 1/4 teaspoon salt
    - 1/4 teaspoon baking powder
- **For the Cheesecake Layer:**
    - 8 ounces cream cheese, softened
    - 1/3 cup granulated sugar
    - 1 large egg
    - 1 teaspoon vanilla extract

## Instructions

1. **Preheat Oven:**
    - Preheat the oven to 350°F (175°C). Grease an 8x8-inch baking pan.
2. **Make Brownie Batter:**
    - In a saucepan, melt the butter. Remove from heat and stir in sugar, eggs, and vanilla. Mix in cocoa, flour, salt, and baking powder until just combined.
3. **Prepare Cheesecake Layer:**
    - In a bowl, beat cream cheese, sugar, egg, and vanilla until smooth.
4. **Layer and Bake:**
    - Spread half of the brownie batter into the prepared pan. Top with cheesecake mixture, then swirl with remaining brownie batter. Bake for 30-35 minutes. Let cool before slicing.

## S'mores Dip

**Ingredients**

- 1 cup semi-sweet chocolate chips
- 1 cup mini marshmallows
- 1/2 cup graham cracker crumbs
- Graham crackers or fruit, for dipping

**Instructions**

1. **Preheat Oven:**
     - Preheat the oven to 450°F (230°C).
2. **Layer Ingredients:**
     - In a baking dish, spread the chocolate chips evenly. Top with mini marshmallows and sprinkle graham cracker crumbs on top.
3. **Bake:**
     - Bake for 5-7 minutes or until the marshmallows are golden brown. Serve warm with graham crackers or fruit for dipping.

# Chocolate Dipped Oreos

## Ingredients

- 1 package Oreo cookies
- 1 cup semi-sweet chocolate chips
- Sprinkles (optional)

## Instructions

1. **Melt Chocolate:**
    - In a microwave-safe bowl, melt chocolate chips in 30-second intervals, stirring until smooth.
2. **Dip Oreos:**
    - Dip each Oreo into the melted chocolate, allowing excess to drip off. Place on a parchment-lined baking sheet.
3. **Add Sprinkles:**
    - If desired, sprinkle on top before the chocolate sets.
4. **Set:**
    - Refrigerate until the chocolate is firm.

# Chocolate Chip Banana Bread

## Ingredients

- 2 ripe bananas, mashed
- 1/2 cup unsalted butter, melted
- 1 cup granulated sugar
- 2 large eggs
- 1 teaspoon vanilla extract
- 1 teaspoon baking soda
- 1/4 teaspoon salt
- 1 1/2 cups all-purpose flour
- 1 cup semi-sweet chocolate chips

## Instructions

1. **Preheat Oven:**
   - Preheat the oven to 350°F (175°C). Grease a 9x5-inch loaf pan.
2. **Mix Wet Ingredients:**
   - In a bowl, mix mashed bananas, melted butter, sugar, eggs, and vanilla until smooth.
3. **Combine Dry Ingredients:**
   - Add baking soda and salt, then mix in flour until just combined. Fold in chocolate chips.
4. **Bake:**
   - Pour batter into the prepared pan and bake for 60-70 minutes or until a toothpick comes out clean. Let cool before slicing.

## Chocolate Cake Pops

**Ingredients**

- 1 chocolate cake, baked and cooled
- 1 cup chocolate frosting
- 1 cup semi-sweet chocolate chips (for coating)
- Lollipop sticks

**Instructions**

1. **Prepare Cake:**
   - Crumble the cooled chocolate cake into a large bowl. Mix in frosting until fully combined.
2. **Form Balls:**
   - Roll mixture into 1-inch balls and place on a baking sheet. Insert lollipop sticks into each ball.
3. **Chill:**
   - Refrigerate for at least 30 minutes until firm.
4. **Melt Chocolate:**
   - Melt chocolate chips in a microwave-safe bowl. Dip each cake pop into the melted chocolate, allowing excess to drip off.
5. **Set:**
   - Place pops upright in a foam block or in a cup to set.

## Chocolate Waffles

### Ingredients

- 1 3/4 cups all-purpose flour
- 1/3 cup unsweetened cocoa powder
- 1 tablespoon baking powder
- 1/2 teaspoon salt
- 2 tablespoons granulated sugar
- 2 large eggs
- 1 3/4 cups milk
- 1/2 cup vegetable oil
- 1 teaspoon vanilla extract

### Instructions

1. **Preheat Waffle Iron:**
    - Preheat your waffle iron according to manufacturer instructions.
2. **Mix Dry Ingredients:**
    - In a large bowl, combine flour, cocoa powder, baking powder, salt, and sugar.
3. **Mix Wet Ingredients:**
    - In another bowl, whisk together eggs, milk, oil, and vanilla.
4. **Combine:**
    - Pour the wet ingredients into the dry ingredients and stir until just combined.
5. **Cook Waffles:**
    - Pour batter into the preheated waffle iron and cook according to manufacturer instructions. Serve warm with syrup or whipped cream.

## Chocolate Peanut Butter Smoothie Bowl

**Ingredients**

- 1 frozen banana
- 1 cup almond milk (or milk of choice)
- 2 tablespoons unsweetened cocoa powder
- 2 tablespoons peanut butter
- 1 tablespoon honey or maple syrup (optional)
- Toppings: sliced bananas, granola, chocolate chips, and chopped peanuts

**Instructions**

1. **Blend Ingredients:**
    - In a blender, combine the frozen banana, almond milk, cocoa powder, peanut butter, and honey (if using). Blend until smooth and creamy.
2. **Serve:**
    - Pour the smoothie into a bowl and add your favorite toppings, such as sliced bananas, granola, chocolate chips, and chopped peanuts.

## Chocolate Silk Pie

**Ingredients**

- **For the Crust:**
  - 1 1/2 cups chocolate cookie crumbs
  - 1/4 cup unsalted butter, melted
- **For the Filling:**
  - 8 ounces cream cheese, softened
  - 1 cup powdered sugar
  - 1/2 cup unsweetened cocoa powder
  - 1 teaspoon vanilla extract
  - 1 cup whipped cream
- **For Topping:**
  - Additional whipped cream and chocolate shavings (optional)

**Instructions**

1. **Prepare Crust:**
   - Preheat the oven to 350°F (175°C). Mix chocolate cookie crumbs and melted butter in a bowl. Press into a 9-inch pie pan and bake for 10 minutes. Let cool.
2. **Make Filling:**
   - In a bowl, beat cream cheese, powdered sugar, cocoa powder, and vanilla until smooth. Fold in whipped cream.
3. **Assemble:**
   - Spread the filling into the cooled crust. Chill for at least 2 hours.
4. **Serve:**
   - Top with additional whipped cream and chocolate shavings if desired.

# Chocolate Caramel Tart

**Ingredients**

- **For the Crust:**
    - 1 1/2 cups graham cracker crumbs
    - 1/4 cup unsweetened cocoa powder
    - 1/4 cup sugar
    - 1/2 cup unsalted butter, melted
- **For the Filling:**
    - 1 cup heavy cream
    - 8 ounces semi-sweet chocolate, chopped
    - 1/2 cup caramel sauce
    - Sea salt for topping

**Instructions**

1. **Prepare Crust:**
    - Preheat the oven to 350°F (175°C). Combine graham cracker crumbs, cocoa powder, sugar, and melted butter. Press into a 9-inch tart pan and bake for 10 minutes. Let cool.
2. **Make Filling:**
    - In a saucepan, heat heavy cream until just boiling. Remove from heat and add chopped chocolate, stirring until smooth. Add caramel sauce and mix until combined.
3. **Assemble:**
    - Pour the filling into the cooled crust. Chill for at least 2 hours or until set. Top with sea salt before serving.

## Chocolate Chia Seed Pudding

**Ingredients**

- 1/2 cup chia seeds
- 2 cups almond milk (or milk of choice)
- 1/4 cup unsweetened cocoa powder
- 1/4 cup maple syrup (or honey)
- 1 teaspoon vanilla extract

**Instructions**

1. **Mix Ingredients:**
    - In a mixing bowl, whisk together chia seeds, almond milk, cocoa powder, maple syrup, and vanilla extract until well combined.
2. **Refrigerate:**
    - Cover and refrigerate for at least 4 hours or overnight, stirring occasionally, until the mixture thickens.
3. **Serve:**
    - Divide into serving bowls and top with fruits, nuts, or granola if desired.

# Chocolate Hazelnut Mousse

## Ingredients

- 1 cup heavy cream
- 1/2 cup chocolate hazelnut spread (like Nutella)
- 2 large eggs, separated
- 1/4 cup granulated sugar
- 1 teaspoon vanilla extract

## Instructions

1. **Prepare Base:**
    - In a mixing bowl, whisk the egg yolks and sugar until pale and thick. Stir in the chocolate hazelnut spread and vanilla extract until smooth.
2. **Whip Cream:**
    - In another bowl, whip the heavy cream until soft peaks form. Gently fold the whipped cream into the chocolate mixture.
3. **Whip Egg Whites:**
    - In a clean bowl, whip the egg whites until stiff peaks form. Gently fold the egg whites into the mousse until no white streaks remain.
4. **Chill:**
    - Spoon the mousse into serving cups and refrigerate for at least 2 hours before serving.

# Chocolate Banana Cream Pie

## Ingredients

- **For the Crust:**
    - 1 1/2 cups crushed graham crackers
    - 1/4 cup sugar
    - 1/2 cup unsalted butter, melted
- **For the Filling:**
    - 1 cup heavy cream
    - 1 cup chocolate pudding (store-bought or homemade)
    - 2 ripe bananas, sliced
    - Whipped cream for topping

## Instructions

1. **Prepare Crust:**
    - Preheat the oven to 350°F (175°C). Combine graham cracker crumbs, sugar, and melted butter in a bowl. Press into a 9-inch pie pan and bake for 10 minutes. Let cool.
2. **Assemble Filling:**
    - Spread the chocolate pudding evenly over the cooled crust. Layer with sliced bananas. Top with whipped cream.
3. **Serve:**
    - Chill for at least 1 hour before slicing and serving.

# Chocolate Ganache Tart

**Ingredients**

- **For the Crust:**
    - 1 1/2 cups all-purpose flour
    - 1/4 cup cocoa powder
    - 1/4 cup powdered sugar
    - 1/2 cup unsalted butter, cold and cubed
    - 1 egg yolk
    - 1-2 tablespoons cold water
- **For the Ganache:**
    - 1 cup heavy cream
    - 8 ounces semi-sweet chocolate, chopped
    - 1 teaspoon vanilla extract

**Instructions**

1. **Prepare Crust:**
    - Preheat the oven to 350°F (175°C). In a mixing bowl, combine flour, cocoa powder, and powdered sugar. Cut in butter until crumbly. Add egg yolk and water until dough forms. Press into a tart pan and bake for 15 minutes. Let cool.
2. **Make Ganache:**
    - In a saucepan, heat heavy cream until just boiling. Remove from heat and add chopped chocolate, stirring until smooth. Stir in vanilla.
3. **Assemble:**
    - Pour ganache into the cooled tart crust. Chill for at least 2 hours or until set.

# Chocolate Flan

**Ingredients**

- **For the Caramel:**
    - 1 cup sugar
    - 1/4 cup water
- **For the Flan:**
    - 1 can (14 ounces) sweetened condensed milk
    - 1 can (12 ounces) evaporated milk
    - 4 large eggs
    - 1/2 cup unsweetened cocoa powder
    - 1 teaspoon vanilla extract

**Instructions**

1. **Prepare Caramel:**
    - In a saucepan, combine sugar and water over medium heat. Cook until sugar dissolves and turns a golden brown. Quickly pour into a round flan mold or baking dish, tilting to coat the bottom.
2. **Blend Flan Mixture:**
    - In a blender, combine sweetened condensed milk, evaporated milk, eggs, cocoa powder, and vanilla. Blend until smooth.
3. **Bake:**
    - Pour the flan mixture over the caramel in the mold. Place in a larger baking dish filled with water (water bath) and bake at 350°F (175°C) for 50-60 minutes. Cool and refrigerate before serving.

www.ingramcontent.com/pod-product-compliance
Lightning Source LLC
LaVergne TN
LVHW081329060526
838201LV00055B/2535